SHIRLEY ISHERWOOD

Illustrated by Stephen Player

OXFORD
UNIVERSITY PRESS

OXFORD
UNIVERSITY PRESS

Great Clarendon Street, Oxford OX2 6DP

Oxford University Press is a department of the University of Oxford.
It furthers the University's objective of excellence in research, scholarship,
and education by publishing worldwide in

Oxford New York
Athens Auckland Bangkok Bogotá Buenos Aires Calcutta
Cape Town Chennai Dar es Salaam Delhi Florence Hong Kong Istanbul
Karachi Kuala Lumpur Madrid Melbourne Mexico City Mumbai
Nairobi Paris São Paulo Shanghai Singapore Taipei Tokyo Toronto Warsaw

and associated companies in Berlin Ibadan

Oxford is a trade mark of Oxford University Press
in the UK and in certain other countries

First published 2001

British Library Cataloguing in Publication Data
Data available

ISBN 0 19 915970 X

Printed in the UK by Ebenezer Baylis & Son Ltd

Available in packs

Year 6 / Primary 7 Pack of Six (one of each book) ISBN 0 19 915971 8
Year 6 / Primary 7 Class Pack (six of each book) ISBN 0 19 915972 6

This book is dedicated to
Jennifer Rebecca Howarth Gillian Shirley Burrows
Charlotte Rebecca Burrows Olivia Burrows
Lewis Gregory Burrows

To my dear friend John Gilboy, for his unfailing support during the writing of this book – and on countless other occasions

Contents

1
Mousie

I do not talk to other people very much. I answer their questions, I try to smile and be pleasant, but I am always afraid that I won't tell them the thing they want to hear. I am also afraid of what they might ask. I can talk to Mousie more easily than I can talk to people. But Mousie has been with me for a long time.

Doctor Hill suggested that I might find it easier to write. I said, "Who would I be writing for?" And she said, "For you. It would be like writing letters to yourself."

I thought it was a crazy idea, but did not say so. It wouldn't be quite so crazy, I told myself, if I wrote the letters to Mousie, for Mousie at least was someone else. Not a real someone else that's true, but I had made him into a character, I'd put words into his mouth, imagined how he would behave. To me he was real.

It seemed far more sensible to write to him rather than to myself, and without thinking I said this to Doctor Hill.

To my surprise she neither laughed nor looked cross. "Write to Mousie by all means," she said. She was adding something to her notes at the time, and did not look up.

'Suppose," I said, fearful, but wanting to test her, wanting to see how far I could go with this joke. "Suppose he writes back?"

She did look up at this, her grey eyes calm and steady. "That's a nice idea, Eva," she said.

* * *

So I took a thick writing book, and my blue pen, and sat Mousie on the pillow beside me on the bed, and began to write. I wrote until the daylight began to fade, but I did not stop to switch on my lamp. Mousie's bright, black eyes gleamed at me in the half-light. They had a sharp, clever look, as if he already knew what I had written, as if he knew exactly where I had begun the story.

At suppertime, Mrs Aden laid my plate and knife and fork on a folded white cloth, on a corner of the table in the big, warm kitchen. She did not try to talk to me, or encourage me to talk to her.

I was grateful for that.

While I ate I thought about what I had written. I had not described the place where I now live, or the people here. My letters are to Mousie and he already knows what this place and these people are like.

He knows about the past too, of course, but that's different. For, almost as soon as I had begun to write, I knew what Doctor Hill hoped would happen.

For a long, long time it has seemed as if monsters walked behind me. They were evil and ugly and terrifying and to turn and look at them would be to invite their wrath, which was terrible. Doctor Hill said that the monsters were really the things that had happened to me and Jacob – to hundreds of children like us.

Now, I knew that with the letters to Mousie I would be taking my first glance. I wondered, if Mousie replied, would it be his first glance too?

Then I realized that Mousie had never looked away, that he knew and understood far more about what had happened to us than I had ever guessed.

2
Jew, Jew, Jew

After supper, I cleaned my teeth, put on my pyjamas, and lit the little bedside lamp in my room. I curled up on the bed, with Mousie beside me, and read what I had written.

Dear Mousie,

My father gave you to me on my birthday. I don't remember how old I was. But I remember that I liked you best of all my presents. My father said, "I saw him in a toyshop window, looking all forlorn, and I said to myself, 'that mouse belongs to Eva!'"

My big present was a doll, Donna Clare. She had perfect limbs and cold, blue eyes and I hated her. I held you close, as though you would protect me from her.

My mother, who had chosen Donna Clare for me, was disappointed. She walked the doll towards me, making her bow and say things in a high, squeaky voice.

I made no reply. I had already discovered that when you were unsure, or afraid, it was best to keep silent. I had said nothing to my parents about what was happening to me at school; the jostling, which was supposedly accidental, followed by the grinning, insincere apology, the foot jerked out suddenly as I passed between the rows of desks, so that I stumbled and fell. And the whispered word, "Jew, Jew, Jew..." Sometimes the sound followed me all day.

My best friend, Clara, thought that Donna Clare was beautiful. At my party, I saw her make the doll's stiff legs march like the legs of a storm trooper.

Soon, all the children joined in the game. They

stamped round the room, laughing and shouting.

Some of the adults were alarmed, but others said, "They're just children. They're having fun. Children are great mimics."

Love,

Eva

3
Mrs Aden

After I had finished writing, Mrs Aden looked round the bedroom door. "Time to put your light out, Eva," she said. She glanced towards my blackout curtains, but I had drawn them tight together, so that not a chink of light would show. "Goodnight," she said and smiled. "Sleep tight, mind the bugs don't bite." She always said that.

In the night, I awoke and heard planes flying overhead, but the warning siren was not sounded. Just before I went back to sleep I thought I heard the sound of the pages of my writing book being turned. In the morning, I found that Mousie had written a reply to my letter.

Dear Eva,

I, too, heard the whispering. I was in your school bag, the one that Grandpa bought that smelled so beautifully of leather, and with the straps with brass buckles which jiggled and made a noise like little bells when you ran to school.

I lay at the bottom with your books and pencils, your crayons and your India rubber, and the sweets that Grandma made and hid as a surprise. I sniffed the scent of the orange, and the clean smell of the folded handkerchief that your mother put there, fresh every morning. And I remembered the words of your father, "that mouse belongs to Eva!" I was happy then.

But a mouse knows what is happening through sense of smell and sense of hearing; a mouse does not have to see. In the dark of the bag I began to smell fear and I heard the

"Jew...Jew...Jew...". The sound and the smell fitted together as though they were one thing. What made the sound was the thing that felt the fear.

Love from

Mousie

It was written with my blue pen, in nice big letters. All through that day at school I thought about the last line of the letter.

At teatime, when I returned to the house, I found Mrs Aden reading a letter from her husband. She was crying as she read, and at first I thought she had received bad news, but it was simply that she was so relieved to hear from him. He was away, fighting in the army, but she didn't know where.

Some of the pages of the letter had thick, black lines drawn on them, blocking out the words where he had perhaps written hints to let her know where he was. But I saw all the kisses at the bottom of the page – there were no black lines through those. I wished that I had a letter from my parents, or my grandparents, but the place on the kitchen dresser where Mrs Aden kept the mail was empty. I looked every day, but the letters never came.

That night before supper, I tried to write to Mousie again, but this time I couldn't.

Mrs Aden sang as she served the supper. The food was good, but I couldn't eat very much of it. Mrs Aden told me bits of news from her husband's letter, she was so eager to share her happiness.

But I was sad at the sight of the empty place on the dresser, and because I seemed no longer able to write to Mousie.

When I went back to my room, I found a letter from him on my pillow. Again it was written in big letters with my blue pen. Mousie himself sat on my pillow and watched as I read.

Dear Eva,

I was sitting on your desk when your teacher, Miss Bergen, said, "Eva, to the front of the class please!"

She often did this; you were her best pupil. You took your essay book from your bag, thinking that she would ask you to read aloud.

But instead she stood you in front of the blackboard and began to chalk words over your head. THIS IS A JEW she wrote. You didn't know what she had written. How could you know?

But I saw the faces of your classmates as they read the words. Some looked dismayed, but many had the sudden alert look that I have seen on the face of a cat when it scents its prey.

And the scent that I had caught before came back, the smell of fear, and with it now the smell of hate.

Frida Hegel, who sat in the front row, jumped up and shouted, "Filthy Jew, filthy Jew!" and threw a book at you. It hit you on the forehead, and you flung up your arms to protect your face.

I don't know what happened next. I was knocked down and lay under your desk, seeing only feet running and scuffling, and hearing the shouts. Then Miss Bergson's voice said, "Enough, enough!" and your hand picked me up and put me back into the blackness of your bag. I lay under the pencils and papers. I looked for a sweet but there were none that day. I nibbled a piece of orange peel instead.

After a while I heard the squeak of your new patent shoes as you ran home, heard the jingle of the little brass buckles of your bag, heard your father singing as you entered the house.

Ach, du lieber Augustine, Augustine,
Augustine,
Ach, du lieber Augustine, all is gone...

Love from

Mousie

I picked Mousie up and began to cry. I couldn't stop. Between sobs I hiccuped loudly, so loudly that Mrs Aden heard and came into my room.

"Eva," she said, and put her arm round my shoulder, but I just kept rocking back and forth, holding Mousie. After a few moments she left me and went to her neighbour, Mrs Lark, to ask her advice. Mrs Lark said, "Warm milk with a spoonful of brandy!"

They brought the drink to my room, and sat on the edge of my bed as I drank it. It made me sleepy, and I lay down and listened to the sound of them leaving, quietly closing the door behind them.

I awoke some hours later. Mousie sat on my pillow. I took my book and my pen and began to write.

Dear Mousie,

When I left school that day, I saw Clara standing by the gate with a group of girls. Their heads were together and they were talking about me I knew, for one after another turned her head and then quickly turned away again.

I felt like a thing made from wood, and walked slowly across the playground. Then Clara broke away from the group and began to come towards me and the feeling vanished. It returned a second later; someone reached out an arm and pulled Clara back. The group moved closer together, the voices sank lower, almost to whispers. Suddenly they ran. After a moment, and with one last glance at me, Clara ran after them.

My father, as you said, was singing *Ach, du lieber Augustine*. when I reached home. He always sang this song. It was our favourite. He sang the song and gave me a sandwich which I ate in the window seat of my room while doing my homework. This is what we did every day, first the song and the sandwich and later dinner and perhaps a visit from Grandma and Grandpa.

I didn't tell my father about what had happened. My hair covered the bruise on my forehead. I felt as though it hid a dreadful secret, a shameful thing.

As I sat in the window seat and ate my sandwich, I suddenly remembered going for a drive with my grandpa when I was quite small. We drove to the countryside, and he stopped the car at a crossroads. "Which way Eva, to the left or to the right?" he asked.

I pointed to the right, and Grandpa turned the car. "Now, if we come to a horrid place and get eaten by bears it will be all your fault," he said.

"Suppose we come to a nice place?" I asked.

"Ah, that will be because of my cleverness in letting you choose," he said.

We arrived at the outskirts of a village. A sign stood by the roadside and Grandpa turned the car round very quickly before I had time to read it.

"What did the sign say?" I asked.

"Bear Town," said my grandpa. "If we had gone there nothing would be left of us by now save a tiny bone, which they overlooked and my gold watch, which is inedible."

That made me laugh. How safe and happy I felt with Grandpa.

I know now that the sign had said: "Jews Not Welcome". I saw many such signs later.

Love,

Eva

4
Clara

There was a raid that night, but I only half-awoke. I felt myself lifted from my bed by Mr Lark, and carried down to the cellar of the house, which had been made into an air raid shelter.

They sang while in the shelter, Mrs Aden, Mr and Mrs Lark, and whoever else wished to join them; but Mr Lark was often away, for he was a fireman. They sang: *Roll out the barrel*, and *Keep the home fires burning*. But that night they didn't sing because I was sleeping; I half-awoke once or twice and heard the soft murmur of their voices.

I awoke fully in the early hours of the morning, and staggered up the cellar steps, leaning against Mrs Aden. At the top I realized that Mousie had been left alone throughout the night, and I ran to my room, and hugged him.

He had written another letter to me; my book lay propped open at the page. But Mrs Aden was calling for me to wash and dress and to come down to eat.

"We have eggs, Eva!" she called excitedly up the stairs. "Eggs for breakfast! What a treat." Eggs were rare, but sometimes a neighbour who kept hens gave us one or two. She sounded so pleased that I couldn't keep her waiting, and hurried down as quickly as I could.

She placed a brown egg before me in an eggcup shaped like a chicken. "That was mine when I was a little girl," she told me.

It was nice, sitting there with the sun shining through the window. As I ate, I wondered what the world had been like when Mrs Aden was a child. After breakfast I went back to my room, and read the letter from Mousie.

Dear Eva,

I was sitting on the window seat that evening. I heard your parents quarrelling, but even with my keen mouse-hearing I couldn't make out all the words. But one word I heard clearly above all the others; *Kindertransport, Kindertransport* – what a strange word it was. The sound of it frightened me.

Then I saw Clara and her mother. They were walking on the other side of the street. Two girls from your class were walking towards them, soft leather cases under their arms, on their way to their music lessons. They passed Clara and her mother with scarcely a nod of recognition.

Yet they were children who often played with you and Clara.

Clara's mother looked disturbed and puzzled, but I understood why they acted in that way. Clara had tried to defend you; Clara was the friend of a Jew.

Clara's mother stopped for a moment and gazed after the girls. Clara hung her head. Then they crossed the street and came to the front door of the house.

A few moments later, the door of your room opened, and there she stood, pretty Clara, unsure and nervous but trying to smile. "I didn't throw things, Eva," she said. "Some of the others did, but I didn't. I tried to stop them, but I couldn't."

You turned your head away from her. You wouldn't look at her.

"I was frightened," she went on. "I didn't know what was happening. I ran back to my desk and put my fingers in my ears and closed my eyes..."

You just stared out of the window and held me tight. Clara waited for a little longer, then left.

But she spoke the truth, Eva. I saw her feet as she ran back to her desk, her feet in the shiny black shoes like yours with a strap and a button. They twisted together as she sat, like two frightened little animals trying to comfort one another.

Love from

Mousie 

I sat down on the edge of the bed, and replied to the letter at once.

Dear Mousie,

She lied. Clara lied. Clara always tells lies to save herself. Clara would say anything, do anything to stay out of trouble.

Love,

Eva 

I ran downstairs and sat with Mrs Aden all evening. We listened to the radio while Mrs Aden knitted a scarf in khaki wool.

"Did you have a best friend when you were my age?" I asked. The question came out in a rush, surprising me; I don't usually ask questions.

Mrs Aden looked up from her knitting and smiled. "Oh, yes," she said, "I had a best friend. Maggie and Annie, the terrible twins they called us."

"I was, and still am, Maggie," she added, going back to her knitting.

When I went back to my room, I found this written in my book.

Dear Eva,

It wasn't just the black shoes. Remember mouse-hearing, how sharp that is? From a tangle of shouts and yells, like drawing a straight thread from a great knotted ball of yarn, I drew out the voice of Clara screaming "No! No! No!"

Love from

Mousie

5
The End of School

Dear Mousie,

I wish I could have believed Clara when she came to my room that night. I wish I could have said, "Oh, Clara!" and hugged her. Then at least I would have one good memory of a school friend, someone who had tried to defend me. Perhaps if we had had the chance to see each other again, I might, in the end, have believed her. But I never went back to school. Clara told her mother what had happened, and her mother told my parents.

We never met again, although I used to catch a glimpse of her on her way to and from her lessons. Sometimes I saw the whole class, walking in a crocodile, on their way to the park or the museum. Clara would raise her head quickly, and look at my window. We made no sign that we had seen one another.

Then one morning, my father came into my room. "Eva," he said, smiling, "you are going to school – a very small private school." He sat down on the window seat beside me. "In fact," he went on, "there will only be two students."

I was happy, excited. My days had been long and dull. I put my books, and pencil, and you, Mousie into my bag, and we set off down the street. My mother had tried to teach me but her lessons always turned to talk about how wonderful things had been before the Nazis. The lessons, too, were almost always interrupted by visitors. My mother made coffee for her guests and herself. It wasn't real coffee, but made, someone told me, from acorns. As they drank the awful stuff, my mother and the visitor sat close together and talked in low voices.

They spoke of neighbours taken suddenly in the night; of how the sound of jackboots was heard and then the loud knock on the door, how some struggled and fought, and how some went meekly, knowing that there was nothing they could do.

I was pleased to be going away from all this. But my happiness faded when we reached the house. It was shabby, dirty, and my teacher was a tired-looking young woman.

The other pupil was a boy, a little older than me – Jacob...

I had to stop writing my letter at this point for the siren sounded again, and once more we made our way down into the cellar.

This time I was not drowsy with milk and brandy, and took Mousie with me. Mrs Lark was with us, and an elderly lady who lived further along the street. The noise of the bombs sounded close. Mrs Aden knitted very quickly, and the elderly lady murmured a prayer. Mrs Lark, I knew, thought of Mr Lark, who was out in the streets somewhere with bombs falling round him.

"He'll be all right," said the elderly lady, who I was later to call Miss Doris. "The Good Lord will look after him."

I wondered why, if the Lord was good, he allowed bombs to be dropped on us why he allowed any of the dreadful things that happened in the world.

But the all-clear came before long, and we went back upstairs. Mrs Aden made a pot of tea, and soon Mr Lark came into the kitchen, tired, dusty, his face smeared with dirt.

I went to bed and tried to finish my letter, but I was too tired. I just wrote "Love, Eva," and fell fast asleep.

6

Jacob

Both Mrs Aden and I overslept the next morning. I scrambled into my clothes and ran downstairs. There was no brown egg for breakfast, only heavy, grey, wartime bread spread with margarine. But there was honey; Mrs Aden's mother was a beekeeper and sent us jars. She lived in the country, where Mrs Aden had lived as a child. Someday, said Mrs Aden, we would visit her. I looked forward to that.

I reached school just as the bell rang to call everyone in from the playground. I liked being at school, but I couldn't concentrate that day.

My mind was full of Jacob. We had been together for long, so much had happened to us, good things as well as bad, that it was impossible to think of him not being with me.

Sometimes I imagined that I would turn a corner and see him coming towards me. "Eva, Eva!" he would say and take my hand and hurry us away to the next episode in our lives. Mrs Aden, the songs in the shelter, my room with my little lamp where I wrote to Mousie, all would be gone like a dream.

But it was Jacob who had gone, Jacob who was the dream.

When I reached the house, I began another letter to Mousie.

Dear Mousie,

Do you remember Jacob? Do you remember how bossy I thought him? Do you remember how scornful I was of everything, the squalid room, Miss Ember in her shrunken sweater, the pencils that were only stubs, the scraps of paper – I hated it all...

...and especially Jacob.

"Well, Eva," said Miss Ember, 'this is your classmate. You must try to do as well as he does, though I doubt you can. Jacob is very clever."

I could see nothing special about him; he was just a good-looking boy with thick, black hair. I took my things from my bag, and set them out on the table that served us for a desk. I sat you down in front of my books, and at once he snatched you up with a snort of derision...

I didn't finish my letter, for I was called away by Mrs Aden. She stood in the kitchen, smiling, with a basket of gooseberries on the table before her.

"Jam, Eva," she said, "I'm going to make jam! Would you like to help?"

I sat at the table, and topped and tailed the fruit. It had been brought by Mr Lark, who, when he wasn't fighting fires, worked on his allotment where he grew fruit and vegetables.

We worked all evening, Mrs Aden and I. Neither of us had made jam before. "There's more to it than I thought," said Mrs Aden. But the rows of glass jars with their little paper tops looked impressive, and we felt pleased with ourselves.

We had supper and listened to the wireless for a time, then, feeling sleepy, we made our way upstairs. "Good night, sleep tight," said Mrs Aden as we went to our rooms. "Mind the bugs don't bite."

But I didn't go to sleep for some time. There was another letter waiting for me.

Dear Eva,

I certainly do remember Jacob! (read the letter on my pillow) Snatched up by the bow round my neck, swung back and forth by my tail, then tossed into the air – wouldn't you remember such things if they'd happened to you? Oh, the sight of that laughing face, as down I came, and your hands reaching up to catch me! But he was taller than you. He always caught me. You tried to push him aside, but he was too strong.

I was giddy with twirling through the air. When at last he gave me back to you, and you put me in my place on the table, I couldn't sit up. You tried to set me upright, but each time I fell over sidewise.

This undignified game took place every day until Miss Ember put a stop to it. "There will be no more playing with this toy!" she said, and bundled me into a drawer.

This toy! Me, Mousie, who had been your loving and devoted friend for so long, who knew you better than anyone, even your beloved Papa!

I was nothing more to them than a piece of grey velvet, a scrap of ribbon...

In the darkness of the drawer I heard you shouting, "Give him back to me! I hate it here! I hate you! This isn't a real school and you're not a real teacher."

"Sit down," said Miss Ember, her voice ice-cold. "I am a teacher. I am a good teacher. I am also Jewish, like you and Jacob. Because of that, neither of you can go to school, and I am not allowed to teach.

"You find this place disgusting. But I would like to tell you that this is not my home. My home was taken from me and given to an officer of the SS. My home was as fine as yours. The only reason why your home has not been given to the SS is because your father pays bribe money. But when the money is gone, what then, Eva?"

There was a long silence after this. When at last Miss Ember spoke her voice was softer. "I ought not to have said the things I did. You are children, you ought to be able to enjoy as much of your childhood as is left to you."

"I am not a child," said Jacob.

Miss Ember opened the drawer and took me out. She straightened my ribbon bow and my ears and then set me down in front of you. You looked pale and subdued. Jacob sat at your side, calm and in control. Looking at him I thought, despite the silly games with me, he was, as he said, no longer a boy but a man.

Love from

Mousie

7

The Man in the Alleyway

Dear Mousie,

It is very early in the morning. All night I dreamt of Jacob and Miss Ember, not about what happened but a lovely story where she took us both to her home, and we all three drifted through beautiful rooms, as effortlessly as spirits.

What really happened was, to make up our quarrel and to prove that I truly did think that she was a teacher, I asked her if she would teach me French.

She was pleased, partly because it showed that I trusted her and partly because it meant that my father would pay more money, which she badly needed.

Jacob said that he did not want to be taught French, that he already had enough languages with German, Hebrew and Yiddish.

My lessons were to be in the evening. My father took me to Miss Ember's house and sat drinking *ersatz* coffee in a small café nearby until I was ready to go home.

The first French words which Miss Ember taught me were *mon petit souris gris* – my little grey mouse. They were in fact the only French words she taught me. On our way home, a riot broke out. We heard the sound of shouts and the breaking of glass. My father held my hand tightly, and said, "Hurry Eva, hurry!"

But the crowd came up behind us, and pulled us apart. They were waving sticks, many held bricks and stones. I was carried forward with the movement, and turned to try to make my way back to my father. But I couldn't see him, nor could I fight my way through. It was as if I was helpless in a strong sea.

Then the crowd parted, moved on, and I was left alone on the pavement. I stood in front of Cohen's bakery shop, dazed and frightened. A moment later, a group of young men, some only a little older than Jacob, ran down the street. They carried stones and bricks that they threw at the bakery windows.

They shouted and laughed as the windows shattered, and they danced back and forward, their faces flushed with pleasure, as though they were at a carnival and what they were throwing were harmless paper streamers. I stood, unable to move, and they danced round me, as though they didn't see me.

But someone did see me and rescued me. An elderly man in a long black coat and a black deep-brimmed hat took my arm and hurried me down the street, to the opening of a narrow alleyway. "Go, go!" he said, urgently.

I was reluctant to go down the alley. I wanted to find my father. "Go!" the man said again, and I took a few hesitant steps. Then I looked back and saw that the youths who had smashed the bakery window were standing at the alley's entrance, under the yellow street light. The man stood some little way between the youths and me. "Go!" he said again, "Run!"

I turned and ran. As I went, I heard the sound of bricks and stones falling against the pebbles of the alley. When I reached the end of the alley I stopped and looked back. The youths had gone and the man was crouched against the wall. As I gazed at him, he fell sideways slowly and lay still.

Then I heard my father's voice calling me. "Eva! Eva!" I ran to him, and took his hand. We walked quickly down the street.

"Are you all right?" he asked, as if nothing more had happened to me than a slight tumble. I knew instinctively why he did not show his concern; we had to look as though what had taken place had nothing whatsoever to do with us. But it had everything to do with us, I knew.

I didn't tell him about the man in the alley.

Love,

Eva

8
"How Can I let her Go?"

Dear Eva,

Soon after, I began to hear quarrelling voices again and the strange word that had frightened me before – *Kindertransport*.

Love from

Mousie

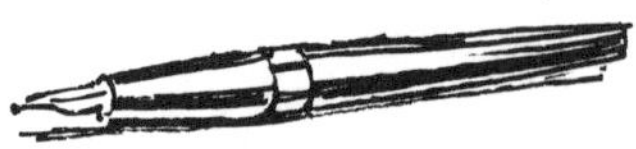

Dear Mousie,

This time I heard it too. They quarrelled so hard that they forgot to lower their voices. My mother said, over and over, "She is my child, my only child. How can I let her go? We might never see her again."

My father said, "It is the only thing to do... the only thing."

Love,

Eva 

Dear Eva,

When your father came to explain what was to happen that day, I was afraid I was going to be left behind. What was I, after all, but a scrap of grey velvet and a ribbon? How could I tell myself that I was anything more? My tail was a piece of string, my eyes black beads; but I felt that my heart was real. It beat fast, as if it would break.

You sat on the edge of your bed, and as your father spoke, I saw your hand reach out without looking at me. I knew then that we would always be together.

Love from

Mousie 

9
Into the Country

Mrs Aden and I tried the jam next morning. It was a great success. After breakfast the postwoman brought the mail. There was no letter for me, and no letter from Mrs Aden's husband, Jim, but there was a lovely fat envelope from Mrs Aden's mother.

"You must share it with me," said Mrs Aden and we sat crushed together in the old armchair, and read the closely-written pages.

Mrs Aden's mother wrote about her cats, Buffy and Matt, and the old donkey, Moses, who lived in the paddock at the bottom of her garden. She wrote about what was happening in the village. "We're all collecting old pans, to make into a Spitfire!"

Mrs Aden and I looked at one another. "An aeroplane," she said. "From old pans!" We laughed and turned to the next page.

"Mrs Fellows' son, who was reported missing, has been found, safe and well in a prison camp in Germany.

I went down to the hives in the evening and told the bees. I usually only tell them news about close family, but I have known Jamie Fellows since he was a small boy. He helped me with my hives when I first became a beekeeper..."

I loved the idea of talking to bees, but wondered how you would do it.

"The fruit trees are full of plums," went on the letter. "Do try and come for a visit, then you can take some home to bottle. And I would love to meet Eva!"

"Shall we?" asked Mrs Aden. "Would you like that?"

"I'd like it more than anything in the world!" I said.

* * *

There were posters everywhere at that time. One of them asked sternly: "Is Your Journey Really Necessary?"

"Yes, it is!" said Mrs Aden, and we hurried to the ticket office and bought our tickets.

The carriage was packed with soldiers, land girls, girls in the uniform of the ATS and just travellers like me and Mrs Aden. Everyone was cheerful, or pretended to be.

The journey took all afternoon and most of the evening. The train stopped twice because of air raids. It reminded me of the train journey with Jacob, but I didn't want to think of that; I wanted to think only about the plum trees and the donkey and the hives of bees, about everything that Mrs Aden's mother had written about in her letter.

At last I fell asleep. When I first awoke, I imagined that I was with Jacob on the train that was taking us to Dachau. I gave a cry and struck out wildly. Mrs Aden wrapped her arms tightly round me and held me until I wakened fully. "You were dreaming," she said.

The train drew up at the village station at Highfields and we got out. Mrs Aden's mother was waiting for us with a little pony and trap and we made the journey to her cottage in the velvety darkness.

Mrs Aden and her mother exchanged their news, and I sat listening to the sound of the jingling harness, the hoot of an owl, and the soft breeze in the trees.

My suitcase lay at my feet and I held Mousie in my hand. I wondered if he knew that owls ate mice. I tucked him under my cardigan so that he would feel safe.

When we reached the house, I saw the dark shapes of the hives at the bottom of the garden and asked Mrs Aden's mother how you talked to bees. She said that she would show me in the morning; that she would have to tell the bees that there was a stranger in their midst otherwise they might fly away.

"Not that you'll be a stranger to them for long," she said and added, "You've never been a stranger to me. I feel I know you so well through Maggie's letters."

Mrs Aden showed me to my room. It had a sloping roof, a little window and a bed with a thick crotchet cover. I thought that I would sleep well, but I dreamt again of Jacob.

10
On the Train

Dear Mousie,

My father paid for Jacob's ticket for the train that was to take us away from Germany. He did this so that I would not be alone with strangers, and so that I would have someone to look after me.

I wish that I could tell him how well his money was spent, how, of all the many things that he bought for me, two became the greatest comfort and loves of my life – Jacob and Mousie.

For Jacob did think that he had been bought. He quarrelled with his mother over this in the kitchen of their house, while my father and I waited in the next room.

"But you *must* go," his mother said. "It is a wonderful chance. I will follow when I can – I promise."

"When?" Jacob asked coldly. "How?" As I listened to his voice, I knew that my father too had lied when he had made the same promise to me. "Mummy and I will follow as soon as we can."

"And Grandma and Grandpa?"

"Yes, yes, we will all be together again."

'Liar!" I thought now, sitting in Jacob's house, and took my hand from his.

Jacob's mother came with my father to the station to say goodbye. My own mother was too upset; for days she had kept to her room, weeping. Jacob and I leant from the carriage window and waved for as long as we could see the two of them standing on the platform.

The train was packed, mostly with children and women. I felt tired and sick. Jacob found seats for us, and I sat with my suitcase at my feet and with Mousie in my hand. A small boy sitting next to me wanted to play with Mousie. He reached out his little hand, and his mother smiled at me, but I snatched Mousie away. I had no one else now who was my own, and I didn't want to risk losing him.

Jacob, who sat opposite, gave me a scornful look.

We travelled for what seemed like days. Children cried, quarrelled, the carriage grew hot, and there was nothing to eat or drink.

"Where are we going?" I asked Jacob, but he just shrugged. "Well, Jacob Marks," I told myself, "there are some things you don't know, after all," and fell to thinking about our lessons with Miss Ember. How she had praised him, and how he had preened like a peacock! He was the most conceited boy I had ever met, and now I was trapped on a train with him, being taken to, no one knew where, except that once there we would be safe.

I thought too about the day when we had both arrived for our lessons, me with my father and Jacob alone, as always, only to find Miss Ember's room locked.

"She's been taken by the SS," a neighbour told

us in a low, excited voice. "She taught Jews," he added.

Before my father hurried me away, Jacob's eyes met mine, and I knew that we both had the same thought. The neighbour was not appalled by the fact that Miss Ember had been arrested, but by the fact that she had taught Jews.

I wondered where my father was now, and if my mother still wept in her room. Then I fell asleep and was woken by the slowing down of the train. The woman next to me looked anxious and held her little boy tight. Voices were heard in the crowded corridor. "They're stopping the train at the border. We're being taken to Dachau."

I turned to Jacob. For a brief moment, he looked afraid, then he took my hand, and flung open the carriage door on the far side of the compartment. "Jump!" he said, tersely. I stood, frozen with terror.

"Do it!" he said. I obeyed, and together we rolled down the steep embankment. Others jumped behind us.

The noise alerted the military guards, and they released their dogs. I heard cries and screams,

but Jacob pulled me on. "Don't look back," he said, and again I obeyed. After that train journey I almost always obeyed him.

Love,

Eva

11
Telling the Bees

It was early morning when I wrote that letter to Mousie. I sat by the window and gazed out over the garden, the hives, and the paddock where the donkey scratched his back against the fence. Mrs Aden's mother appeared in the garden. She looked up and beckoned to me.

"I'm going to tell the bees about you," she called. I ran downstairs and followed her to the bottom of the garden. The cats came with us, their tails erect and waving gently to and fro. Moses brayed loudly when he saw us, like a greeting.

"He's telling us, 'Good morning! I'm hungry!'" said Mrs Aden's mother.

We reached the bees and she bent her head close to the hive.

I hoped that she wouldn't say what so many people said when they introduced me. "This is Eva. She has had a dreadful time; she has seen so many terrible things. She is a brave child."

I had not thought about this until the moment when I bent my head with hers and heard the buzzing from within the hives. I knew that bees would not expect me to tell them anything about the things that had happened, but I didn't want to hear those words again. They made me feel a fraud. I was not brave. Jacob and Mousie knew how frightened I had been, how much I had cried.

But Mrs Aden's mother just said, "This is Eva, our friend. She's come for a visit."

When I went back to my room after breakfast, I found Mousie's reply to my letter.

Dear Eva,

You obeyed Jacob except for the time when you rolled to the bottom of the embankment and then discovered that you had dropped me!

How frantically you began to search, with Jacob, almost as desperate, trying to pull you away.

And I was so near, almost by your foot, lying in the prickly bushes. But it was looking for me that saved you both. I saw a guard come to the edge of the embankment and look down. He noticed neither you nor Jacob. You were both on your hands and knees, searching the undergrowth. You had told Jacob that you would not leave until I had been found. How fierce you were! And how impressed he was by your determination – although you did not notice; you were too intent on your search.

You found me just as the guard turned away convinced that no one had escaped from the train successfully.

Love from

Mousie

P.S. Oh, what would have happened if you had not found me!

Dear Mousie,

But I did find you, and I shall never lose you again.

Jacob and I walked all night. In the early morning we came to an overgrown wood. It was a good place to be; it was quiet and the air around us was still and calm. We sank down on to soft moss and slept. When we woke we realized how hungry we were.

"If this was a kid's story," said Jacob with a wry grin, "I'd make a bow and arrows from twigs, shoot a rabbit, make a fire, and we'd eat."

"You'd have to have a knife to skin the rabbit," I told him.

"Oh, I'd be the kind of kid that always had a

knife," said Jacob. He pulled me to my feet and we began to walk.

We had not gone far when we saw Sara and Samuel watching us from between the trees. They were younger than Jacob and me, and their hands were full of root vegetables, turnips, parsnips and carrots. Clearly, they had just dug the vegetables up, for their clothes were daubed with mud. Sara wore a little gold Star of David round her neck.

"Jew. *Juden*," said Jacob softly, pointing to himself and to me. He approached them as though they were little forest animals who would dart away at the first sign of danger. Which of course they did.

Jacob followed, racing after them, leaping over creepers and brambles, and leaving me behind, clutching you. I wanted to cry out to him, "Don't leave me!" but was afraid of who might hear me.

I waited for what seemed a long time, and then I saw him coming towards me through the trees. He was crunching a carrot and ambling along as though we were on a picnic instead of fleeing for our lives.

I was so angry that I could have hit him, but he just stood there, grinning. He brought his other hand out from behind his back and presented me with a carrot as though it were a bunch of flowers.

Then he hurried me through the wood and I ate the carrot as I went. It was very good.

Soon, we came to where Sara and Samuel knelt in the opening of a dugout. It was quite large, and had a heavy, grassy flap held back by stout branches. Sara and Samuel's parents crouched at the back of the dugout, like animals in a burrow.

"I'll make one these for us!" said Jacob. I didn't doubt for one moment that he could.

Love,

Eva

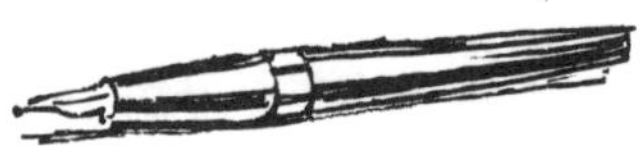

12

The Burrow in the Wood

I remembered our time in the wood so vividly that I wanted to write it all down at once. Somehow, it was easier at the cottage to think of all that had happened. It didn't make me feel as afraid as when I had remembered at other times. Sitting in the garden, hearing the voices of Mrs Aden and her mother as they picked the ripe plums in the little orchard and with Mousie and the cats, Buffy and Matt, beside me, I felt safe.

Mrs Aden's mother thought at first that I had been given homework. She said, "What a shame! The child's on holiday!"

But Mrs Aden explained. Mrs Aden had known from the first about the letters; Doctor Hill had told her everything and neither she nor her mother ever asked to see what I had written. Doctor Hill had promised me that no one would ever see it if I didn't want them to.

I fell asleep under the trees, thinking how happy I was. When I woke up I found Mousie's letter.

Dear Eva,

It was just as well that no one had to read it! You wrote so quickly when you described the time in the wood that your handwriting was almost unreadable! I saw little of what happened in those first few days.

Sara noticed me and my still-jaunty red bow. She came closer and closer, ignoring her mother's order to come away. How right you were when you likened them to animals in a burrow! Her mother's voice was like the bark of a fox.

Her father's voice was gentler. He came and

took his little girl's hand and led her away. She turned her head and gazed at me as she went. I thought that later you might relent, and at least let her hold me for a while. Instead, you found a hiding place for me, and all I saw for some time, at least through the daylight hours, was the leaves and grass with which I was covered. And the occasional spider.

You have no idea how much a spider tickles when it walks over your nose.

Love from

Mousie

Dear Mousie,

I'm sorry about the spiders. But I'll tell you about our first days in the wood.

We slept under the trees that night. When we woke, mist was drifting between the trunks, and birds were waking and beginning to sing.

"We'll be all right here, Eva," Jacob said.

"How do you know?" I asked.

"I just do," he said. "I feel it."

He stood up and stretched and began at once to search for a place to make our shelter. He soon found a good spot. But after he had dug for a time, using a piece of wood and sometimes his hands, the earth just fell back into the hollow that he'd made.

Again and again he scooped out the hollow, but every time the earth refilled it. Sara and Samuel came to watch, standing some distance away from us. Their parents came, too. When I turned my head to look at them, I saw the woman say something to the man; her expression as she spoke was hard and cold and I knew that she did not want us to stay. None of them wanted us, except perhaps Sara.

At that time I imagined that they had the whole peaceful wood to themselves and didn't want to share it with anyone, the way I didn't want to share you, Mousie.

I didn't know about the Cohens, the Goldmanns, the Himmelfields, and all the others whose names I never learned, who lived in holes, tree-houses and man-made burrows, even in the hollow trunks of trees. They all came to watch, silently, as Jacob dug frantically in the earth.

I couldn't bear to see him so angry and humiliated. I knelt at his side and began to claw at the dirt. We didn't speak or even look at one another.

We only became aware of Luke when we saw his two great boots planted one on either side of us. He set me on my feet as easily as if I had been you, Mousie; Jacob he let rise of his own accord. Then he turned and faced the watchers.

"They're children," he said, jerking his thumb first at me and then at Jacob. "Jews, like us. If they leave here and get caught, then we'll get caught, too."

I saw Sara's father say something to his wife. She nodded. He went to the dugout and came back with a spade. Others brought tools for digging and stout tree branches and began to help us. When the hollow was deep enough, the sides were lined with the wood so the earth could no longer fall back.

Jacob uprooted a small bush and we replanted

it at the opening; once you scrambled past it, the branches closed over the entrance. Little golden shafts of light shone through the leaves.

We sat side by side. Jacob had regained his pride, he had worked hard, Luke had said so; the other men too treated him not as a boy but as a man like themselves. Now we looked at one another and grinned. "You're like an old badger," I told him.

"And you're a little mole," he replied.

We were Badger and Mole for the rest of our stay in the wood.

Love,

Eva

Mrs Aden and her mother came from the orchard carrying the baskets of plums. I jumped up to help carry them into the kitchen. I left Mousie behind in the grass, and saw the cats touch him inquisitively with their noses. "How surprised he'll be!" I told myself. "First spiders and now cats."

13
Hunters and Hunted

I helped Mrs Aden's mother cook supper that night. She was surprised at how good I was with vegetables, washing them, scraping them clean. "I'm good at digging them up, too," I told her.

"Oh, did you have a vegetable patch?" she asked.

"No," I said, "I dug them up in fields. It was often all we had to eat." It was the first time I had ever offered any information about what had happened, and I spoke without thinking. I saw Mrs Aden's mother pause with her hands in the mixing bowl.

Mrs Aden was knitting a khaki balaclava, which is a sort of helmet that fits over the head and neck and has a slit for the eyes. She too paused for a second. Then she held up the needles, and sighed. "Do you suppose that anyone will ever want to wear this?" she asked – she was not a good knitter. They both knew that I wouldn't say more.

But they'd been so kind, I felt that I ought to at least try to explain to them why I couldn't talk about what happened. "Mrs Aden…" I began. They both looked puzzled for a second, and then laughed.

"You really can't go on calling Maggie 'Mrs Aden'," said Mrs Aden's mother. "From now on, we're Maggie and Bea."

So I didn't say anything more about our life in the wood; in fact, I forgot all about it for a time. Bea brought out her photo albums. There were photos of Maggie in her Brownie uniform, and on the beach kneeling before a sandcastle. There were photos of her with Annie, her best friend. Looking at them, I thought of Clara.

I slept soundly that night. It was only when I woke that I remembered I had left Mousie outside in the garden. I ran outside in my pyjamas and found him – I also found a rather damp letter.

Dear Eva,

I waited for you all night. The cats prowled back and forth. What disdainful creatures they are – hunters too. But they didn't try to meddle with Me. They understood that I was no ordinary mouse. But they are no respecters of property, as witness the paw prints on my letter.

Watching them come through the long grass carrying pitiful little bundles of fur – you won't like to read those words I know, but why should I spare YOUR feelings? You forgot all about mine! – watching them, I say, I remembered Luke and Jacob coming through the trees, carrying the limp bodies of rabbits.

What a hunter Jacob became, and how you wanted to hunt with him, confident that you could do as well as he. And how angry...

Oh, really, what is the use of trying to finish this letter?

Love from

Mousie

Dear Mousie,

I'm sorry! It was so nice sitting at the kitchen table with Bea and Maggie, looking at the photos, and when I thought about Clara I didn't feel angry. That made me happy. Perhaps the war will be over soon and we can meet, and I can tell her that I know she didn't throw things at me.

Then I was sleepy and Bea bundled me off to bed. She says, "Goodnight, sleep tight, mind the bugs don't bite!" just as Maggie does.

Yes, I remember Jacob and Luke going out hunting and coming back with rabbits. I remember how upset I was by the little furry bodies – and how quickly I got used to it.

I became used to stealing vegetables, too. I went with Sara and Samuel to where the farmer's fields adjoined the wood. There was a crop of carrots in one, and potatoes in another. Beyond, and not far from the farmhouse, was a vegetable patch.

One day, Samuel, thin as a starved rat, and as quick, scurried over the fields and returned with his small hands full of vegetables.

When it was discovered what he had done, he was soundly scolded. He stood, holding radishes, young onions, lettuces, with the proud look of the successful hunter-gatherer; a look which changed to one of shock and bewilderment when his parents shouted at him.

"Don't you understand?" his father said. "A few carrots from a field – who will miss those? But vegetables disappearing from someone's plot will be noticed, and they will look for the thief."

Samuel dropped the vegetables and scrambled into the dugout, pulling down the grass flap. He stayed there all day.

In the evening, when Jacob and Luke returned, they were told what had happened. Luke went to the entrance of the dugout. "Who brought these? What bold hunter found these?" he asked in his booming voice. "If there's one thing I love, it's young onions!"

A second later, Samuel's face peered out.

"*You* brought them!" said Luke. "Then you must hunt with Jacob and me tomorrow!"

Samuel's face lit up. But I was annoyed, and jealous. Neither Jacob nor Luke ever suggested taking me with them.

The vegetables that Samuel stole from the patch tasted very good indeed. We shared them out as best we could. The families we knew were the Cohens, the Goldmanns, the Himmelfields. They were pleased to share in the spoil. But Samuel's father had been wrong when he said that vegetables from a field wouldn't be missed.

One morning, Sara and I saw the farmer in his field, shading his eyes with his hand as he gazed towards the wood. Sara and I stood as still as mice, hidden in the shadow of the trees until he turned and stumped away.

Soon after, we saw him on the very edge of the wood. He looked this way and that, but didn't come any further.

We talked about the farmer that night. "Perhaps he is a kind man. He knows we're here, but he won't tell anyone..." said Mrs Cohen. Her voice tailed off, for neither she nor anyone else believed that the farmer was a kind man.

"A man with compassion would leave something for us," said Luke.

We didn't see the farmer for the next few days, but each time I neared the edge of the trees I grew afraid, thinking that he might suddenly appear.

Sara and I began to make our way further and further along the edge of the wood, taking vegetables from parts of the field we had never been before.

And then one morning, there he was, so suddenly it was as if he'd sprung from the earth. He was grinning, and his teeth were long and yellow; my mind seemed to fix quite calmly on that detail.

"Little ladies!" he said, bending to speak to us, for he was very tall. "Little gypsies of the wood! Take what you want! Take it!" He waved his hand over the field, as if offering his entire crop.

When neither Sara nor I moved he dug his hands into the soil, pulling up vegetables and thrusting them at us. We took them and ran.

"Perhaps he is a good man after all," said poor Mrs Cohen. She looked at me hopefully, and at the food we had brought. But for the rest of the morning I felt uneasy. In the afternoon I went to look for Jacob and Luke.

Love,

Eva

Dear Eva,

You took me with you, tied round your waist. You didn't usually take me when you went through the wood, and I thought how glad I was that you didn't. It was no way to travel, bounced up and down on your hip as you ran!

But I sensed your fear. I knew who we were running to, but I didn't know from what. Then, just as you found Jacob setting his traps, I saw the soldiers coming over the farmer's field.

They were armed, their guns held at the ready. They saw you and Jacob and Luke, who was some little way from us, a dead rabbit in his hands.

I saw Jacob's hand come down and grab yours. I heard his voice. "Run!" The path and the trees swayed and tilted before me as we went.

The shot was loud. It echoed through the entire wood, and I heard you cry "Luke!"

You stopped and turned, and I saw him lying in the ferns, the rabbit still in his hand.

Love from

Mousie

Dear Mousie,

We ran into the shelter of the trees. They grew thick in that part of the wood. I heard a whimpering sound and wondered who was making it. I thought perhaps it was you, and held you close to comfort you. Then Jacob's hand came over my

mouth, and I knew that it was me. "Hush, Mole," he whispered in my ear.

We stayed hidden in the trees until night fell. When at last we returned to the camp, there was no one there. The dugouts had been found and destroyed, the Cohen's hideaway, and the places that the Goldmanns and the Himmelfields had made for themselves, all were smashed, destroyed. But our burrow was still there. I crept in and curled up, and at once fell asleep.

When I woke, it was morning, and Jacob was pushing aside the branches of the bush and entering the burrow. I saw that he had Luke's big hunting knife in his hand.

"So?" he said, "Luke has no use for it."

He was right, of course, but it seemed such a cold, hard thing to have done, and I knew that Jacob was neither cold nor hard, though he often pretended to be.

I nodded and lay down again. My head ached.

Jacob said, "I must go out again. Here's Mousie to keep you company till I get back."

Love,

Eva

Dear Eva,

I knew that you were ill. I tried to comfort you. I sang *Ach, du lieber Augustine* as your father used to do...

Ach, du lieber Augustine, Augustine,
Augustine,
Ach, du lieber Augustine.
All is gone...

Love from

Mousie

Dear Mousie,

I heard you singing; then your voice became the voice of my father. I was in our house once more, and he was giving me my sandwich as he always did, but when I reached out for it he took the plate away.

Love,

Eva

14
The Picture on the Wall

I remember very little of being ill. I seemed to sleep and wake then sleep again. Each time I woke I was aware of Jacob's presence, if not in the burrow, then somewhere near. Mousie was always there where I could see him. It was like dreaming one dream after another; some were good and some were not.

Then one morning I awoke fully, with a clear head and a horrid thirst. Jacob was sitting nearby, his knees bent under his chin, and his hands clasping Mousie.

"Hello," he said, and grinned, "welcome back!"

I was very weak but we decided that after another day's rest we would leave the forest. I asked Jacob if he knew where we were and he brought out a tattered map. I knew at once that it had belonged to Luke.

But we weren't the only ones to take from the dead. That evening as we lay in the burrow, we heard the sound of footsteps. A beam of light from a torch could be seen through the leaves of the bush at the entrance.

I thought that the soldiers had returned, and I gave a cry, and scrambled to the back of the burrow. Jacob put out his hand and touched me. "Quiet, Mole," he said. "It will be all right." Then he peered through the branches.

It was the farmer who had betrayed us to the Nazi soldiers, and his wife. They were searching the camp, looking for anything valuable or useful. There was nothing, and after a while they left.

I realized then that the farmer must have discovered where our camp was some time ago. Perhaps he had come at night when we were sleeping, to look at the dugouts and burrows and tree houses, planning how he would bring soldiers to kill us all.

"You look pensive, my dear," said Bea, pausing by the tree, where I sat with Mousie and the cats, her laundry basket full of clothes to be hung on the line. I didn't know the word, pensive, and must have looked puzzled.

"It means to think deeply, to be a little sad in your thoughts," she said. Then it must have seemed to her that her words were very like a hidden question. "I don't mean to pry," she added, hurriedly.

I jumped up to help her with the laundry. "You weren't prying," I said. "I wasn't thinking of anything, really."

Together we pegged the sheets and pillowcases on the line with Bea's fat wooden pegs.

As we worked, I wondered what she would have said if I had told her what I was thinking about.

* * *

Dear Eva

I don't think that she would have said anything at all. She would have just listened. She would have not wept over you. That's what frightens you, the idea that someone will cry and their tears will make your own tears start. That's why you don't talk about any of it. That's why you find it easier just to think about it, or write to me.

Love from

Mousie

P.S. You left me with the cats again, but no matter.

* * *

I found this letter when I came back from a walk to the village with Bea. I answered it at once.

Dear Mousie

I think that your remarks are very silly, and I have a good mind to leave you with the cats forever. Or better still, put you in the paddock with the donkey!

Love,

Eva

That evening Bea taught me how to make bread. I loved everything about it, the smell of the frothy yeast, the kneading, the waiting for the loaves with their floury tops to rise in their tins, and the wonderful smell as they baked in the oven.

Maggie knitted the never-ending balaclava. "Maggie makes beautiful cakes, but she can't make bread," said Bea.

"Maggie can't knit either," said Maggie ruefully, holding up the needles. "I've made another hole… I can't imagine how."

Bea took the knitting from her. "You've dropped stitches all over the place," she said.

As I watched their two heads close together, murmuring to one another, I had the sudden memory of watching my grandmother make lace. It was her hobby and I tried to describe to Bea and Maggie how swiftly she threw the bobbins with their beaded ends back and forth over the little pillow on which she worked.

* * *

I hadn't thought about Grandma or Grandpa

for a long time. I scarcely even thought about my father or mother any more.

The loaves were taken from the oven, tipped from their tins and set to cool, covered with a white cloth.

"You can have a slice with honey in the morning," Bea told me.

I went out into the garden and collected Mousie. When I was in bed, I wrote him a letter, the first I had written for some time: I didn't count the little note in the garden with the threat to leave him with the donkey.

Dear Mousie,

We left the wood the day after the farmer and his wife searched the camp. I hated leaving our burrow; in it I had felt safe. I liked being Mole and Badger, but now I would have to be Eva again, and Jacob would be Jacob, and not the hunter of the woods, but...

...what would we be?

We walked for a long time, stealing food from fields and orchards. My feet were sore and I was often cold. I don't know how Jacob felt. "It does no good to talk about it," he said, and so I held my tongue. But one day I said, "Oh, Jacob, I can't go any further!" and I really felt that I couldn't.

"Yes, you can," he said. "You must," and he put his arm round my waist and dragged me on. In this way we walked another four miles.

That evening we came to a town. The market was about to close, and stallholders were packing their goods away. Jacob approached a stall on the edge of the market, and took some things from his pocket. I couldn't see what they were for the light above the stall was a dim gas light, and Jacob and the stallholder, a woman, stood close together. She shook her head, and said something to him. Jacob turned and beckoned to me.

"She's going to help us," he said. I stepped back, feeling wary and afraid. I thought, she will be like the farmer offering us his vegetables, only to trap us; but then she turned her head and smiled, and I knew that she wasn't like the farmer at all. She had a lovely smile and a lovely open face, with faint freckles over her nose and big grey eyes.

The woman's name was Elsa, and we helped her to pack up her goods. Just as we closed the last case a man came up and kissed Elsa on the cheek. He was her husband, Otto. He and Jacob took the cases and we all made our way through the dusky streets, like a family returning home after a day at work and school.

Except that we walked more quickly than such a family would have done, and we didn't talk to one another or stop to look into shop windows.

The place that Elsa and Otto gave us was a small section of a bedroom that had been partitioned off with thin board. The opening was behind a chest of drawers. Inside were a mattress and pillows and blankets. We both fell asleep almost at once.

"We'll be safe here, Eva," said Jacob, when we woke in the morning. I felt that he was right, we would be safe at least for a time, but the place didn't make me feel safe, like the burrow had done. I felt trapped.

Jacob left me alone, after we had eaten the bread and cheese which Elsa brought us. He wouldn't tell me where he was going; I later discovered that he went foraging. We had been given a safe place to hide and he didn't want to be a heavier burden on Elsa and Otto than was necessary.

I argued with him that we would become more of a burden if he were caught. But ever cocksure he wouldn't agree with me. Left alone, I wondered why I felt as I did about the hideaway, and thought that perhaps it was because we had helped to make the burrow ourselves, and so it seemed more our own. We always spoke of it as "the burrow" – but what could I call this? "The space?"

One day, turning the mattress to make it more comfortable, I saw a little drawing on the wall. It was done on a loose curling piece of the wallpaper, and it showed a lion tamer and his lion. I knew as soon as I saw it that it had been made by a little Jewish boy; that others had been hidden here before us. But where were they now?

In the long days when Otto and Elsa were away at markets, and Jacob was out foraging, I thought about the little Jewish boy and his picture, and wondered if he was still alive. I hoped so much

that he was. When I looked hard at the picture I could see how cleverly it had been made; how the artist had managed to show a look of love in the face of both the man and the lion with just a few small scribbly lines.

I loved the picture so much that I carefully peeled the piece of wallpaper off the wall. I have it still.

Love,

Eva

15
Maggie and Bea

The next day was Saturday and we began to think about going back to Maggie's house. "Stay till Monday at least," said Bea.

I was on my way to the garden, carrying Mousie and my writing things, and paused to hear Maggie's reply. I was pleased when she agreed, but as I went though the kitchen door I caught the words, "Have you said anything about…" they were spoken by Bea and I somehow knew that they referred to me.

Soon after I had settled under the tree both Maggie and Bea came to join me. "We've been wondering, Eva, if you'd like to live here with me?" said Bea. "That is, until the war's ended, and..." She left the sentence unfinished and I knew she meant until your parents find you – if your parents find you.

I was surprised, and looked from one to the other.

"It's not that I don't want you," said Maggie. "It's just that, well, you seem to be so much happier here."

I thought of the very first night when I had arrived at Maggie's house, with nothing more than Mousie. I could say scarcely a word either of thanks or of greeting. Maggie had been told about me by the lady from the Red Cross, who brought me to her.

Maggie accepted me at once. She put up with being woken night after night by my bad dreams. She didn't ask me what the dreams had been about, nor could I have told her, the details vanished as soon as I woke but left me filled with horror and fear. She just sat with me and told me stories about what had been happening in her day.

Lots of people wanted to meet me at that time. They meant well, they made a fuss of me, trying to make up, if only in a small way, for what had happened. I was invited to children's parties but found them strange, almost unreal. Maggie never made excuses for me, the way that adults do for children who don't behave quite as expected.

I thought about how, if I stayed with Bea, Maggie would be alone in her little house, listening to the news on the radio, waiting for letters. I wasn't wonderful company, but I was someone there.

"No," I said, "I'd rather stay with Maggie. It's not that I've not loved it here, but…" I stopped, not knowing how to say what I felt.

"...I think I would have become happier anyway," I said. "It just happened..."

Both Bea and Maggie hugged me, and went back to the house. I sat leaning against the tree trunk for a while, hearing the faint sound of their voices from the kitchen. Mousie lay in the long grass and looking at him, I thought that his smile, which was permanent (being stitched in black thread) was wider than before, turning up the corners of his mouth in a delighted little quirk.

16
Trapped

Dear Mousie

I'm glad that you're happy, too! How could we not be? Of all the places we have been, this is the best. Apart from my real home, of course, but I can scarcely remember now what that was like. The faces of my parents, and my grandparents are faint, like old photos.

But I can recall Jacob's face as clearly if he stood before me. And I can call up every detail of our last hiding place, "the space" – the chinks of light which shone through the cracks of the board, the musty smell, which made me think of mice in a hole, and the sounds which came from the outside world; the sound of voices, of marching feet, the rumble of traffic when a military convoy passed through.

Bored and anxious, as I lay waiting for Jacob to return from his foraging, for Elsa and Otto to return from the markets, I made up stories from the sounds I heard. The days passed and I forgot their names, they were all so alike.

Until the morning when Jacob and I were woken by the sound of the front door of the house being smashed in. There were loud voices in the narrow hallway, voices that asked questions, demanded answers. Then came the sound of boots on the stairs. The door of the bedroom was flung open. Jacob and I held one another tight, hardly daring to breathe. The bright, narrow shaft of light that fell on Jacob's hand from the chink in the board vanished and re-appeared, as whoever it was in the room strode back and forth.

At last a voice said, "Nothing! There's no one here!" and the footsteps made their way back down the stairs.

After a time, when all was quiet, Jacob crept out from the space and went downstairs. A moment later, I heard him call my name. I went to the top of the stairs and looked down. He was standing at the bottom, and he was deathly pale.

"What is it?" I asked, my voice nothing more than a whisper.

"They've gone," he said. "Elsa and Otto – they've been taken."

I made my way slowly down the stairs. My legs felt shaky and I took hold of Jacob's hand. He held it tightly, and together we went into the kitchen.

The remains of Elsa and Otto's breakfast were scattered across the table; but the two little plates of bread meant for Jacob and me, each plate carefully covered with a saucer, had been left standing on the dresser.

I said, "Jacob, what shall we do?"

"Stay here and manage as best we can," he replied.

"How?" I asked him.

"We managed in the wood," said Jacob. But somehow it seemed less dangerous in the wood.

And in the wood there hadn't been the horrid feeling of being trapped.

He must have guessed what I was feeling. "We won't have to live in 'the space'," he said. "The house has been searched. I don't think the soldiers will come back."

"It's like taking Luke's knife," I told him.

"No it's not," he said. He was no longer pale and his voice was firm. "We have to live somewhere, Eva, and if Elsa and Otto come back we will have kept the house safe for them."

He brought our plates from the dresser. "Eat," he said. But I couldn't.

Love,

Eva

17

Stealing from the German Army

We left the cottage the next day, with the plums and two of the loaves I had helped bake packed in a basket by Bea. “Come back soon!” she called, as the train pulled out of the station. None of us could have guessed just how quickly we were to return.

The journey took most of the day. When we finally arrived home we were greeted warmly by Mrs Lark and Miss Doris.

“I’m driving a wagon for the W I!” Miss Doris told us proudly. “A nice green wagon with hot food for people who’ve been bombed out.”

She looked so bright and energetic that

Maggie and I looked at her in amazement; then we remembered our manners, stopped staring and congratulated her. She bustled off then, as her shift was about to start.

"Well!" said Maggie, after Miss Doris had gone.

"It's made a new woman of her," said Mrs Lark and I realized for the first time that for some people there were certain things about the war that were fun. The realization puzzled me, but I was too tired to think any more about it. I was just glad that we were back.

"Bed!" said Maggie, noticing my yawns.

In bed with Mousie beside me on the pillow, I took my writing book, and began to look back through the letters, to find what had been good in my war. As I read I couldn't believe how much I had written, how much I had remembered.

I was pleased and proud, and sat hugging my knees, thinking that when I was an old lady, my children and grandchildren would read the letters.

Then I thought that perhaps I would never

live to be an old lady – perhaps I would never even live to be as old as Maggie. Children as well as grown-ups died in wars. I felt sad and powerless then, and wrote to Mousie, hoping that it would make me feel better.

Dear Mousie,

Jacob warned me not to go out of Elsa and Otto's house. He said that there were more soldiers about than before. We must come and go only when it was dark.

For a time I was happier just not to be in "the space". I roamed about the house, looking in drawers and in the wardrobe in Elsa and Otto's bedroom, where their clothes still hung on the hangers. I didn't touch anything, except for the photo albums.

I spent hours gazing at pictures of Elsa and Otto, and their friends and relations – although I had no idea which was friend and which was relative. I invented names for them, and told myself stories about them.

Then I began to be aware once more of the

sounds from outside. There were children playing close to the house. They held what seemed to be earnest discussions, sometimes they quarrelled, and they chanted as they skipped rope.

The chant was one which Clara and I knew. We sang it as we skipped rope together, one facing the other. As I listened to the children, I could see her so clearly in my mind's eye.

One sunny afternoon I opened the front door of the house, and looked out. A group of girls was some little distance away and one of the girls saw me. She smiled and beckoned, and after a moment's hesitation, I went to join her.

It was so good to be outside again, to be laughing and skipping in the sun. The rope was held across the width of the narrow street, and we took turns, jumping on one foot and then the other, turning as we jumped.

It was when I turned that I saw Jacob appear at the end of the street. He was carrying an armful of wood, and my first thought was how good it would be to have a fire, for the evenings were growing chilly. Behind him came three young soldiers, scarcely older than Jacob himself. One called to him in a jeering tone. Jacob quickened his step. The solider called again, this time the mocking tone was replaced with one of anger and authority.

Jacob paused. The soldiers came up to him, and began to question him. I was too far away to hear what was being said, but I saw Jacob drop the bundle of wood, and turn out the contents of his pockets. He placed the things in the soldier's hands, and they were passed from one to the other. The voices sounded angrier and became louder, and I heard the words, "Stealing from the German army!"

"Oh, what has Jacob done?" I wondered. The game in the street had stopped, for the girls had seen the soldiers too, and the rope they held lay limp.

One of the soldiers took Jacob's arm to march him away. Jacob broke free and began to run towards me, and the soldier drew a pistol and shot him. He dropped instantly and lay still. The soldier put the pistol back into its holster, and he and his comrades turned on their heels and left. The girls with the skipping rope stood silent for a moment,

then they ran away.

For a time, I stood staring at the body of Jacob and the scattered bundle of wood. Then I went into the house and closed the door.

Love,

Eva

Dear Eva,

You came into the house and curled up on Elsa's big basket chair, your legs bent double, your fists under your chin, like an unborn baby. You made a soft little whimpering sound. I sat on the table, but I couldn't go to you. I thought that you would remember that I was there, and would pick me up so that I could comfort you. I didn't know what had happened. I had just heard the girls' voices, the laughter, the chanting and the shot.

When Jacob didn't return, then I knew.

In the morning, you packed a little bag, and left the house.

Love from

Mousie

Dear Mousie,

I took some clothes that belonged to Elsa, a sweater and a shirt, a pair of shoes and some of Otto's handkerchiefs. I didn't think anyone would mind. I found some money in a drawer and I took that also.

It was early morning when I opened the door and stepped out into the street. It was quite empty – Jacob had gone. I began to walk, with no idea of where I going.

Love,

Eva

Dear Eva,

But you put me in the case, together with the clothes! I lay huddled in the handkerchiefs. I would rather have been tied round your waist, as I was that day in the wood. You had forgotten me. I was lonely.

Love from

Mousie

Dear Mousie,

I wanted to keep you safe! As I walked I thought of you wrapped up amongst Otto's handkerchiefs.

Love

Eva

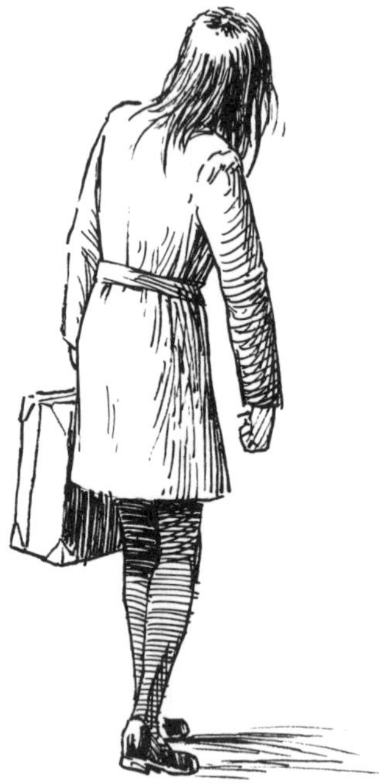

Dear Eva,

I didn't want to be wrapped up. I wanted to be with you!

Love from

Mousie

18
Air Raid

I had just finished reading Mousie's letter when the sirens went and almost at once it seemed, bombs began to fall. Maggie hurried me downstairs but we didn't have time to reach the shelter. There was a great roaring sound, so loud that it hurt my ears, and Maggie bundled me under the kitchen table. Beams of wood from the ceiling, bricks and glass fell down on us.

The lights went out, and we breathed dust. I hugged Maggie tight and felt her trembling. It grew very cold, and I thought of Mousie alone in what was left of my bedroom.

Dear Eva,

But I wasn't in your bedroom. The blast of the bomb bounced me right out into the street! Miss Doris, with her green wagon with the hot food for the homeless, found me sitting on a brick.

"Why, that belongs to Eva!" she said and tucked me into her pocket.

Love from

Mousie

That was how Mousie came back. He was the first thing I saw when Maggie and I were rescued – well, his ears anyway, peeping out from Miss Doris' pocket.

His ears and the two, big steaming mugs of sweet tea that she held in her hands.

We weren't hurt, just dazed, and covered in grit and dust, but the house was unsafe. There was a great hole in the roof and the end wall was cracked. There were no windows left.

The furniture that wasn't too damaged was taken to Mrs Lark's, and Miss Doris's. We packed what clothes we could and Mr Lark clambered over the rubble and found my book and pen.

With just these things, we caught the train back to Highfield and arrived in the early evening.

"Oh, my goodness!" said the station-master, Mrs Potts, when we stepped from the carriage. "Whatever happened to you two!"

"Bombed out," said Maggie.

"Does your mother know?" asked Mrs Potts. Maggie shook her head.

"I've half an hour between trains," said Mrs Potts. "I'll cycle over and let her know."

We sat, leaning against one another on a bench on the platform. It was wonderful to breathe the sweet-smelling country air. I thought, "Soon, I'll see Bea, and the cats, Moses..."

I must have fallen asleep for the next moment, Maggie was gently shaking my shoulder. I stood up, a little shakily and saw, on the other side of the station fence, the pony and trap and Maggie's mother smiling and waving.

When we reached the cottage, we both had baths straight away in the tiny bit of water that was allowed, and Bea brought me a lovely cake of soap to use, the colour of honey and with the most wonderful smell.

"Pears," she said. "That's what it's called. You can't get it any more and I've been saving it for a special occasion."

After our baths we had supper and then we went straight to bed.

"Good night, sleep tight," said Maggie as we went to our separate rooms.

"You forgot, 'Mind the bugs don't bite!'" I told her.

19
Alone

The next morning was sunny and warm. I helped Bea set the breakfast table. A little while later, Maggie came down, yawning, and we sat down to eat.

"Eva was so brave, yesterday!" Maggie told her mother. "We crouched under the table, and I was terrified out of my wits, but Eva didn't turn a hair."

"Yes I did," I corrected her. "I was frightened, but not very much. I've been trapped in an air raid before."

Both Bea and Maggie looked at me.

"In Rotterdam," I said. "Some people

helped me there."

"Oh, my dear!" said Bea.

"But how did you get to Rotterdam ?" asked Maggie.

"I don't know," I said. "After I left Jacob, I just walked." I saw Maggie and Bea glance at one another at this.

"Jacob?" asked Maggie, gently.

"He was my friend," I said. "He looked after me – and then one day, he couldn't anymore..."

I couldn't bring myself to tell them why Jacob couldn't look after me any longer; I couldn't even tell myself. I had almost convinced myself that he had just been wounded, that during the night he had regained consciousness and someone had helped him to a hospital where he got better and that one day we would find one another again.

"It must have been so hard, being on your own," said Bea.

"I don't remember much about it," I said, and it was true.

But that night in bed I began to think about how it had been on the long days when I had walked to the borders of Germany.

Dear Mousie,

I had nothing but the little cardboard suitcase that I had taken from Elsa's house. You were safe inside. No one took any notice of me. Why should they? I was just a girl, going on an errand; or perhaps on her way to spend a night with her friend or her grandparents, since she carried a little suitcase.

I walked until I reached the outskirts of the town and the first farms. When darkness began to fall, I went into a barn, and climbed to the top of the bales of hay.

As I lay there, a farm hand went by the barn door. His dog caught my scent and began to bark. I stared down over the edge of the bales, and the farm hand looked up and saw me. For a moment our eyes met; then he bent, quietened the dog, and went on his way. I felt neither fear at his approach nor relief when he left.

The next day I walked on, and the day after that. All the time, I felt nothing, not even weariness. How restful it is, not to feel; after a while it is as if you no longer exist. I dug up vegetables from fields to eat, as I had done before.

Then I noticed, but with no sense of curiosity, that the roads were fuller than they had been. I came across little groups of people who were walking with cases and bundles; some wheeled barrows or prams.

Occasionally I tagged along with a group – they accepted me, and asked no questions. Sometimes they gave me what food they could afford. No one spoke much, and I thought, "They're like me, they don't feel."

But I did discover from what little talk there was, that they were mostly Dutch and Belgians taking the last chance to return to their homelands.

One afternoon, I came across a car stopped by the road. The boot and the bonnet were open and a man and a woman were peering at the engine.

Without even thinking about it, I climbed into the boot and hid under a tarpaulin. After a few minutes, I heard the sound of the bonnet being closed, and then the boot lid was slammed down.

The car continued on its journey. I pushed the tarpaulin away from my face and lay wondering where I was going, but not really caring. All I wanted to do was to keep moving.

The engine stalled again and a moment later, the boot was opened. The man and I stared at one another, and then he called something to the woman in a language that I didn't understand, winked at me, and covered me up again and closed the boot.

The car started once more, after he had tinkered with the engine again, and didn't stop until we reached the border. I heard guards' voices, and the answering voices of the man and woman. The border guards dismissed us and we travelled on.

I became drowsy with the warmth, and was startled when the boot was thrown open yet again, the tarpaulin removed and a man and a woman stood smiling at me. They were both middle-aged and plump.

They helped me from the boot and settled me on the back seat of the car with my case. They talked excitedly together as we drove on, and even though I didn't understand the language I knew that they were talking about me, for the woman turned from time to time to smile at me. "*Juden?*" she asked, and I nodded.

"Dutch," she said pointing to herself and the man. "Marta – John."

Marta and John lived in Rotterdam. Their house was beautiful, big and old, built of red brick. The rooms were filled with pieces of heavy, highly-polished furniture, each piece laden with ornaments and photos in frames. Sitting at the table, or in the great armchairs, I felt as small as a doll or a tiny child.

But I hadn't realized how thin I had become. The sight of myself in a long mirror gave me a shock.

Love,

Eva

Dear Eva,

I understand how you felt! You sat me down on one of the polished chests, and I saw my reflection, saw at once that my tail was missing. I peered down between my paws and saw my ears, one now gone floppy, and my black-bead eyes. I wondered what I had looked like when I had been new.

Love from

Mousie

Dear Mousie,

Your velvet was silky, not rubbed away in places as it is now. But that doesn't matter, I love you more the way you are. We have meant so much to one another, been through so much together.

What must you have thought of me, with my matted, unwashed hair, my eyes ringed with dark shadows? And how enormous were my knees, sticking out from under my skimpy skirt!

For a time, I stood staring at myself. I thought I reminded myself of someone else, another child, but who? Then I remembered Sara and Samuel. We all had that starved-rat look about our bodies and on our faces an expression that was a mixture of fear and cunning.

I wondered that Marta and John, especially Marta, could be so taken with me, looking as I did, and being almost mute.

After my hair had been washed and trimmed, Marta tied it back with a wide ribbon bow. Then she showed me to John, proud of her handiwork, for I did indeed look better for a bath and some clean clothes.

But I was not a child who looked well in satin bows; I never have been. I think John agreed with this, for he winked at me again, and nodded at Marta, smiling, to please her. He was a great one for winks and smiles. During all the days I spent with John and Marta we talked mainly in winks and smiles since neither knew the other's language.

But the days were not many. Rotterdam was bombed, the centre of the city was laid waste. I crouched beneath the massive mahogany table, as I crouched beneath the kitchen table with Maggie, and heard the house crash down around me. I lay there for a day and a night and on the next morning, rescuers dug me out, and I was given hot, sweet tea to drink.

Marta and John were dead, I knew; I saw Marta's hand reaching out from the rubble. As I drank my tea, I wondered what it was like to die. The thought didn't upset me. I finished my drink, took the satin ribbon bow from my hair, flung it down, and simply walked away. No one noticed me, I was just a girl, clutching a toy mouse.

I made my way to the docks, following the crowds who were making their way there also. I followed a family up the gangplank of the trawler *Princess* as if I were one of them, and sat on the deck, watching the grey waves.

A member of the Red Cross welcomed me to England as I stepped ashore. I could tell her my first name, Eva, and nothing more. That was all that was left of me.

The Red Cross lady took me to Maggie. Later I was taken to see Doctor Hill.

Love,

Eva

20
The Last Letter

I wrote the last letter to Mousie sitting in my favourite spot in the garden. Maggie had gone back to the house, to collect any letters that might have come from her husband. She returned in the early evening, carrying a letter addressed to me. It was from the Red Cross and told me that my mother, my father and my grandmother and my grandfather were alive and well in Lucerne, Switzerland.

"You'll be able to write to them!" said Maggie, beaming down on me.

But my writing book was full. "I'll buy a new one tomorrow!" I thought, and reached up and handed the old book to Maggie. I watched her go over the lawn, then I picked Mousie up from the grass and went down to the bottom of the garden, to the bees.

"Mum and Dad and Grandma and Grandpa are alive..." I told them, then hesitated, unable to say the words that I needed to say.

"...but Jacob's dead."

I thought of the burrow and the sunlight shining through the leaves of the bush. I thought of his courage and his smile.

"Jacob's dead," I said again, and imagined for a moment that the humming in the hives had stopped; but it continued, like the sound of all the summers, and of all things growing. I turned, and followed Maggie into the house.

About the author

At the start of World War Two, a little girl slightly older than myself came to live with my family and me. This was Eva. She had been sent from Germany by her parents, who had no idea when, or if, they could follow her. But they did manage to escape from Germany, and were re-united with Eva through the work of the Red Cross.

Eva's parents spoke often of what had happened to them, but I can't remember ever hearing Eva speak at all. What she experienced as she travelled through Europe remains a mystery. As a child I sat quietly and listened to her parents telling stories which have haunted me all through my life until last year, when I sat down and wrote *Eva*.

Eva really did stand in front of the class, with the words 'This is a Jew' written in chalk above her head. This was in fact the reason why Eva's parents decided to send her away. But, while I invented much of this story, incidents like the ones in the book did happen to many children and so, in a sense, the story is a true one.